MW00449211

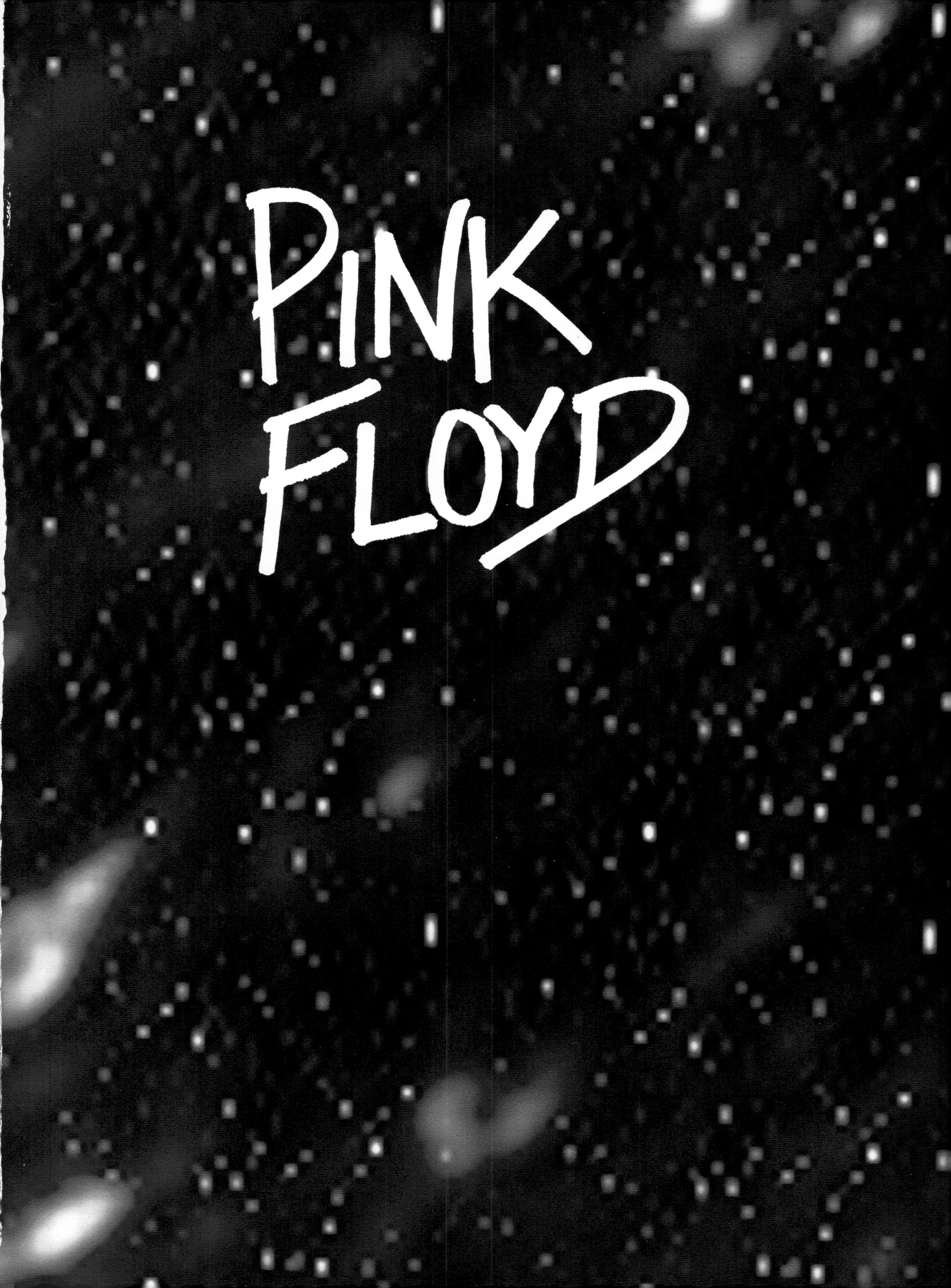
PINK
FLOYD

# PINK FLOYD

WILLIAM RUHLMANN

SMITHMARK
PUBLISHERS INC.

This edition published in 1993
by SMITHMARK Publishers Inc.,
16 East 32nd Street
New York, New York 10016.

SMITHMARK books are available for bulk purchase for sales promotion and premium use. For details write or telephone the Manager of Special Sales, SMITHMARK Publishers Inc., 16 East 32nd Street, New York, NY 10016. (212) 532-6600.

Produced by Brompton Books Corp.,
15 Sherwood Place,
Greenwich, CT 06830.

ISBN 0-8317-6912-2

Printed in Hong Kong

10 9 8 7 6 5 4 3 2 1

For John Mock

## ACKNOWLEDGEMENTS

The publisher would like to thank Elliot Tayman of The Amazing Pudding Magazine, and 'Old Pink' of Atlanta for the generous use of his collection, as well as the many Pink Floyd fans who provided invaluable information and assistance. Thanks also go to Sara Dunphy, the picture editor; Jean Martin, the editor; Don Longabucco, the designer; and Elizabeth A. McCarthy, the indexer.

## PICTURE CREDITS

British Film Institute: pages 41 (all three), 51 (all three), 87.
Camera 5/Klvetmeier: page 10 (bottom).
Carnegie Hall Archives: page 48.
Everett Collection, Inc.: pages 75, 76.
Claude Gassian: pages 2-3, 4-5, 37, 44-45, 46, 47, 52, 53, 54-55, 57, 58-59, 60 (top), 61 (top), 64-65, 79 (both), 80 (top), 84, 85, 86 (both), 90 (top).
Globe Photo/Adam Ritchie: pages 22-23 (all three).
© Arni Katz/Dreamtime Systems: endpapers, pages 1, 30, 40, 42, 49, 50, 62 (bottom), 70, 74, 81, 88 (bottom), 89, 91 (both).
London Features International Ltd.: pages 12, 15, 24, 26.
Kip Lornell/Blues Archives, University of Mississippi: page 20 (top left, right).
Louisiana State University, Special Collections, Hill Memorial Library: page 68.
Robert Minkin: pages 82, 83.
Alex Oliveira/DMI: page 88 (top left).
Photofest: pages 71 (top), 77 (both).
Pictorial Press: pages 6, 14, 18-19, 20 (bottom), 21, 25 (top right), 28, 35; Tony Gale/Pictorial Press: pages 16-17 (all four); Janna/Pictorial Press: pages 8-9; Mayer/Pictorial Press: pages 11, 56, 62 (top), 63, 71 (bottom), 72-73 (bottom).
David Redfern/Redferns: pages 60-61 (bottom).
Relay/Photofeatures; Andre Csillag: page 7 (bottom); S. Emberton: page 69.
Retna Ltd; Lenny Baker: page 90 (bottom right); Adrian Boot: page 29 (top);, Michael Putland: pages 7 (top), 10 (top), 38-39 (both), 80 (bottom left), 88 (top right); Luciano Viti: page 80 (bottom left).
Rex Features: pages 27, 78.
© Mick Rock: pages 13, 29 (bottom), 36, 43.
Elliot Tayman: pages 66-67, 72 (top left).
Baron Wolman: pages 31, 32, 33, 34.

*Previous pages:* Pink Floyd's late-1980s 'Momentary Lapse of Reason' tour, minus Roger Waters, included classic Pink Floyd lighting and visual effects updated for the video age.

*Above:* Pink Floyd during the 1977 'In the Flesh' tour, featuring music from the *Animals* LP.

# Contents

# *Introduction*

In the summer of 1990, two musical events occurred that demonstrated both the ongoing impact of one of rock's most enduring groups and its somewhat confused legacy. On 30 June, a giant open-air concert was held at Knebworth, Hertfordshire, in England. The all-day show featured many of the top names in British popular music over the previous 30 years: Cliff Richard, the Shadows, Status Quo, Genesis, Eric Clapton, Elton John, Paul McCartney, Dire Straits, Phil Collins, Robert Plant, and Tears for Fears. All of them were past winners of the Silver Clef Award, given to those who helped raise money for the Nordoff-Robbins Music Therapy Center. Another past winner was the closing act on this special bill, Pink Floyd, who had been awarded the Silver Clef in 1980.

It was the second time Pink Floyd had played Knebworth, the first being on 5 July 1975, when the group had introduced the music from its upcoming album, *Wish You Were Here*, accompanied by low-flying Spitfire airplanes and other elaborate special effects, plus an enormous sound system that broke down at the start of the show, such that the concert is remembered as a disaster. Knebworth '90 came off better for Pink Floyd, but not much: The group's set was played during a steady rainfall.

The show was the last of 200 concerts played by Pink Floyd during a world tour that had begun on 9 September 1987, nearly three years before. Especially in its later stages, most of the dates on that tour had been played in outdoor stadiums or other open areas, before crowds in numbers up to six figures, and the total gross revenues had reached *nine* figures.

But the Pink Floyd that took the stage at Knebworth in 1990 differed considerably from the band that played

*Left:* Pink Floyd backstage at the Saville Theatre in London on 1 October 1967. Left to right: Nick Mason, Rick Wright, Syd Barrett, Roger Waters.

*Above:* David Gilmour in the studio. Gilmour took the helm of Pink Floyd after Roger Waters left the band in 1986.

*Right:* Roger Waters as he appeared during his charity staging of *The Wall* in Berlin, 21 July 1990.

*Overleaf:* The incredibly elaborate 1990 stage presentation of *The Wall* in Berlin, featuring a wall 550 feet wide and 82 feet high and one of the giant puppets designed by Gerald Scarfe.

*Left:* Roger Waters with Joni Mitchell, who sang 'Goodbye Blue Sky' at the Berlin performance of *The Wall*.

*Left, below:* Fans in Berlin hold the masks used during the 'In the Flesh' portion of *The Wall*, which depicts the transformation of a concert into a fascist rally.

*Right:* Pink Floyd onstage in the 1970s, from the viewpoint of Rick Wright's elaborate keyboard setup. Wright is in the foreground and behind him, left to right, are Roger Waters, Nick Mason, and David Gilmour.

there in 1975, indeed from any Pink Floyd that had played from its formation in 1965 up to the final dates of its previous tour of 1980-81. The earlier band had been a quartet consisting of Syd Barrett (replaced by David Gilmour in 1968) on guitar, Rick Wright on keyboards, Roger Waters on bass, and Nick Mason on drums. The Knebworth '90 contingent contained 13 people. Gilmour was still on guitar, Mason was still on drums, and Wright was still on keyboards (and, though it wasn't apparent to the crowd, on salary rather than in a full partnership with Gilmour and Mason), and each was being doubled (and in Wright's case, tripled) by backup musicians. But Pink Floyd's original bassist, who had been the primary creative force in the band for much of its '70s heyday, and who was, in fact, the writer of many of the songs performed, was absent.

To many longtime fans, that meant the group had no more right to call itself 'Pink Floyd' than a group without Paul McCartney could validly call itself 'The Beatles.' To others, the absence of Roger Waters from the 1987-90 tour and from the group's 1987 album, *A Momentary Lapse of Reason*, marked a welcome return to the slow, extended, ethereal, largely instrumental music that dominated the Pink Floyd sound before Waters began to assert his lyrical dominance in the '70s – to them, Pink Floyd was far more real without Waters than it was with him.

For his part, Waters was very much present at the second Pink Floyd-related musical event of the summer of 1990. On 21 July, three weeks after his former colleagues played in the rain at Knebworth, Roger Waters staged a performance of *The Wall*, the thematic album that is second only to *The Dark Side of the Moon* as the most popular music of Pink Floyd's career, at Potzdamer Platz in Berlin, site of the 'no man's land' that separated the east and west parts of the city until the Berlin Wall came down at the end of 1989.

The connection between the Berlin Wall and *The Wall* (which concerns a psychological barrier surrounding its main character) was tenuous, but in the 10 years since its release, the album had become a rock milestone, and the performance of it served as a benefit for British war hero Leonard Cheshire's Memorial Fund for Disaster Relief. It was an all-star affair, featuring Bryan

Adams, the Band, Paul Carrack, Thomas Dolby, James Galway, The Hooters, Cyndi Lauper, Ute Lemper, Joni Mitchell, Van Morrison, Sinead O'Connor, and the Scorpions, with Waters playing the main role, and it featured ambitious staging that even outdid the series of *Wall* shows Pink Floyd put on in 1980-81.

Both the Knebworth and Berlin concerts not only played to hundreds of thousands in person: They were also broadcast on television worldwide, recorded, and released on albums. They represented crowning achievements for the members of Pink Floyd, even if the achievements were separate. More than 20 years after they turned professional, and more than 15 years after the release of their landmark album, *The Dark Side of the Moon*, Pink Floyd could still command massive attention from a world of rock music listeners.

The shows also marked the end of a period of activity and exposure for the musicians that had lasted several years—now these stars would retreat for a while to consider the future. (Two years later, Gilmour and Mason had turned up only on a home video, driving cars in a Mexican roadrace to the accompaniment of some new Pink Floyd instrumentals; Waters was about to release his third solo album.)

Finally, as one watched and listened, one couldn't help noting, for example, that Gilmour sang the song 'Comfortably Numb' at Knebworth (as at all the late 1980s Pink Floyd concerts) out of the context of *The Wall*, in such a way that its subject — a reluctant rock star being drugged by a doctor to prepare him to go onstage — was lost on listeners who probably thought being comfortably numb was a good condition to be in. But at the same time, one had to recall that it was in fact a song co-written and originally co-sung by Gilmour, and that, however powerful, Van Morrison's rendition in Berlin just didn't sound like Pink Floyd. Such conflicts (and there were many of them) inevitably led the Pink Floyd fan of 1990 to recall that question Waters himself had asked, albeit in different circumstances, 15 years before, and that Pink Floyd fans had been asking at least since 1968 in one form or another: Which one's Pink?

*Below:* Syd Barrett in 1969, after he had left Pink Floyd and as he was preparing his debut solo album, *The Madcap Laughs.*

# *The Piper at the Gates of Dawn, 1964-68*

One of the generalizations made about rock 'n' roll musicians is that they tend to come from poor or working class backgrounds, the better to appreciate the primitive blues and country bases of the music. Robert Johnson grew up poor, and so did Hank Williams; so, in fact, did Elvis Presley. The aspiring rock star is usually thought of as coming from similarly hardscrabble origins, with little formal education, and he achieves his renown by an emotional connection to the music, which itself is thought to be at its best when it is at its simplest.

By the time the second generation of rockers began to gain recognition in the 1960s, this generalization had become less and less true. Mick Jagger was studying at the London School of Economics before turning professional as the singer in the Rolling Stones, for example, and John Lennon's background, like that of the other Beatles with the exception of Ringo Starr, was more middle than working class. But the assumption held on: Note that, as late as 1970, Lennon was calling himself a 'Working Class Hero.' And it also affected the way that critics and historians, who began to apply their crafts to rock from the mid-1960s on, looked at the music. When the American record industry joined with *Rolling Stone* magazine to form a Rock & Roll Hall of Fame in the 1980s, it was apparent that this predisposi-

tion was still in place. The hall requires that its inductees must have made their initial recordings at least 25 years ago, which meant that, when the nominating committee gathered in the spring of 1992 to consider candidates for the 1993 induction, Pink Floyd was eligible for the first time. Despite being one of the most successful acts of its time, the group didn't even come close to being nominated, much less chosen for induction.

But then, Pink Floyd had never conformed to assumptions about what rock music should sound like or who should play it. It was a group that, from the beginning, played what it wanted the way it wanted to, adopting the spirit of experimentation typical of the time in which it emerged in the mid-1960s and adhering to none of the constraints typically imposed by the music industry or the critical community. This meant that it was forced to create its own audience rather than play to an existing one that had been properly primed for it by conventional media. It's no wonder, then, that Pink Floyd's massive worldwide success, which made those record company executives and critics irrelevant, didn't come until six years after its first record was released and, though its audience had been building steadily during that period, took a lot of observers by surprise. For anyone who had been listening, however, it was possible to hear many of the elements that came

*Left:* An early publicity shot of Pink Floyd. Left to right: Rick Wright, Roger Waters, Syd Barrett, Nick Mason.

*Below:* Pink Floyd in 1966, as they were beginning to make their name on the London underground. Left to right: Syd Barrett, Nick Mason, Rick Wright, Roger Waters.

together in *The Dark Side of the Moon* right from the beginning.

The five musicians who constituted Pink Floyd at one time or another in its career did not come from poor backgrounds, and they were not uneducated. Three were born in Cambridge, England: George Roger Waters on 9 September 1943, Roger Keith ('Syd') Barrett on 6 January 1946, and David Gilmour on 6 March 1946.

Though they were close in age, one thing that separated Barrett and Gilmour from Waters was that the two younger men, both the sons of doctors, were born after World War II, whereas Waters was a war baby who suffered the fate of many other war babies: Shortly after his birth, his father was killed in action. This event had a profound impact on him, as he would reveal in his later Pink Floyd work, but even as early as his late teens it

may have helped lead to his activity with the Campaign for Nuclear Disarmament. (Ironically, both Barrett and Gilmour 'lost' their fathers later – Barrett's died when he was 12, while Gilmour's moved to the US when the young guitarist was in his teens.)

After attending Cambridge High School for Boys, Waters enrolled at Regent Street Polytechnic in London as an architecture student, where he met Richard William ('Rick') Wright (born in London on 28 July 1945) and Nicholas Berkeley ('Nick') Mason (born in Birmingham on 27 January 1945), both from wealthy backgrounds, who were also students there. The three played music together as a hobby, then turned to it more seriously as architecture began to seem less interesting a profession.

The first band to feature Waters, Wright, and Mason was Sigma 6, for which Waters played lead guitar,

Wright rhythm guitar, and Mason drums, along with Clive Metcalf on bass and two singers, Juliette Gale (who would later marry Wright) and Keith Noble. They went through changes of name typical of developing groups, calling themselves in succession the T-Set, the Meggadeaths, and the Abdabs. They were calling themselves the Architectural Abdabs when they got their first write-up in *The Regent Street Poly Magazine* in the fall of 1965.

Around the time that article appeared, however, the Abdabs broke up, to reconfigure around the trio of Waters, Wright, and Mason, plus two of Waters's friends from Cambridge who had moved to London: Guitarist Bob Close had begun attending Regent Street, and Syd Barrett had earned a scholarship to Camberwell Art School. David Gilmour, who had become a close friend of Barrett's and helped him learn

to play guitar, was still in Cambridge, playing in a band called Jokers Wild that, initially, showed far more promise than the architects' band at Regent Street.

Though he was joining an existing unit, Syd Barrett instantly became its leader. He renamed the group the Pink Floyd Sound, borrowing the first names of obscure American blues singers Pink Anderson and Floyd Council, and took over as lead singer, lead guitarist (Close left the band, Waters moved to bass, and Wright moved to keyboards), and songwriter. Increasingly, mixed in with the Rolling Stones covers and the versions of 'Louie, Louie' and 'Road Runner' that made up the group's set were the distinctive compositions that would turn up on the first Pink Floyd album and singles. Even the cover songs began to feature long guitar solos full of electronic feedback.

This approach made the Pink Floyd Sound a perfect

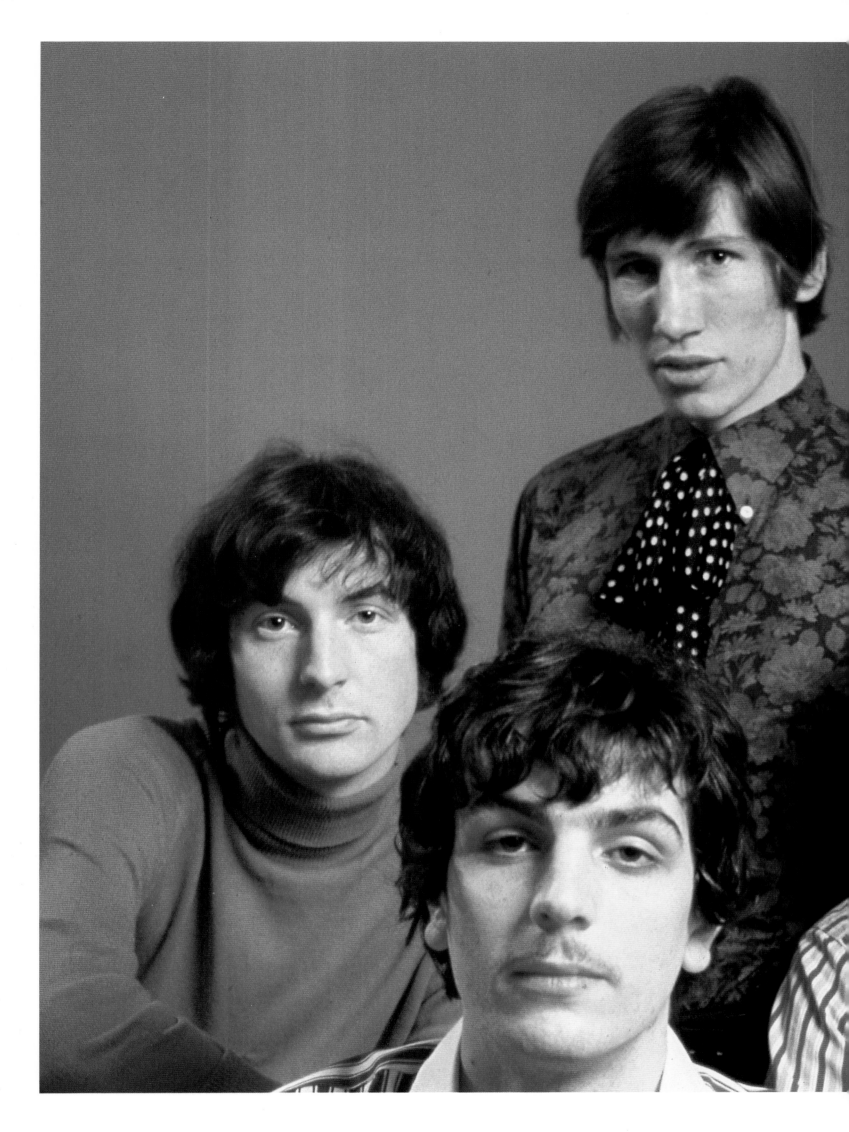

musical accompaniment to a growing 'underground' scene in London in early 1966. Like those in New York and San Francisco, the London artists' community, fresh from its 'swinging' era of 1965, was turning to an experimental period marked by new publications, new clubs, and new music. The term 'underground,' though it had many connotations, was somewhat similar (for music, anyway) to what was being called 'alternative' a couple of decades later – innovative music whose mass commercial appeal was not immediately apparent, but which seemed fresh and exciting to initiates.

The Pink Floyd Sound became the favorite group at gatherings of the London avant-garde arts community, and benefitted from its innovations. In early 1966, they played a show at Essex University at which they performed before the backdrop of a film, the first time Floyd music would be used as literal soundtrack and the first time that a Floyd concert would be dominated not by the group members but by a visual accompaniment. It wasn't long before the group was travelling with its own light show.

The Pink Floyd Sound's first residency in a particular club came at what were called the 'Spontaneous Underground' shows at the Marquee that started in February 1966 (though the Floyd may not have played earlier than March). It was at the Marquee that the band was seen by Peter Jenner, who was part of an independent record production company called DNA. Jenner approached the band with a management offer and the promise that they could be bigger than the Beatles. Roger Waters told him that the four full-time students and part-time musicians would see him after their summer vacation.

By October 1966, the group had returned to playing in London, notably at the mid-October party at the Roundhouse that launched the underground newspaper the *International Times.* By this time, the Pink Floyd Sound was playing songs that might last as long as half an hour and consist largely of improvisations. The London *Sunday Times* called the result 'throbbing music,' while American poet Kenneth Rexroth, writing for the *San Francisco Examiner*, mistakenly reported that the bands for the event hadn't shown up and that a pick-up band played instead. 'Sometimes they were making rhythmic sounds,' he wrote, 'sometimes not.' Far more impressed was *Melody Maker*, which suggested that the Pink Floyd Sound write more of their

own material and 'incorporate their electronic prowess with some melodic and lyrical songs,' in which case 'they could well score in the near future.'

This was singularly prophetic, and such notice helped the students edge closer to becoming professional musicians. On 31 October, they signed an agreement with Peter Jenner and his partner, Andrew King, to form a six-way business organization called Blackhill Enterprises. The new managers' first tasks were to buy the band new equipment (they did, and it was stolen) and to get them a recording contract.

The second task was made somewhat easier because of Jenner and King's production company, which included Joe Boyd, British representative of Elektra Records. After an initial demo proved unsatisfactory, the managers determined to make a record with Boyd producing and then shop it to the record labels.

In the meantime, the Pink Floyd ('Sound' had been dropped officially; 'the' gradually disappeared by the 1970s) was playing frequently around London, notably opening the UFO Club on 23 December 1966. The

*Far left:* South Carolina-based blues artist Pink Anderson, 1900-74.

*Left:* North Carolina-based blues artist Floyd Council, 1911-76.

*Left, below:* An unidentified group plays before the psychedelic light show at the UFO Club in London. The club was where Pink Floyd first made their mark on the London music scene.

*Right:* The office of the *International Times*, though the newspaper on display is a British tabloid decrying the psychedelic scene.

*These pages:* An early Pink Floyd stage appearance dominated by the lighting effects that sometimes made the group itself all but invisible.

club, according to Pink Floyd biographer Barry Miles, 'was to the Floyd what the Cavern was to the Beatles,' i.e., it became identified with them, and was the place where they developed their music and attracted their initial audience.

The group also made its earliest recording actually to be released, appearing in and playing on the sound-track for a 'semi-documentary' film made by Peter Whitehead on the London scene called *Tonite Let's All Make Love in London*. They played the instrumental 'Interstellar Overdrive,' the centerpiece of their con-certs. Whitehead worked on the film for years, how-ever, and it was not until October 1968 that the film opened in London, accompanied by a soundtrack album. Nevertheless, it's notable that, even with its first recording, the Floyd was being associated with film, a relationship that would develop throughout the band's career.

At the start of 1967, the Pink Floyd were on their way. On 1 February, they turned professional (which is to say they dropped out of college), though Mason hinted he just wanted to make a bundle of money and then get back to architecture.

In January, they had begun to play outside London, which occasioned a considerable shock. It was one thing to perform half an hour of guitar feedback before

*Left:* The members of Pink Floyd, sporting the colorful fashions of the day, pose in downtown London in 1967. Left to right: Roger Waters, Nick Mason, Syd Barrett, Rick Wright.

*Above:* Pink Floyd appear on television to promote one of their first singles in 1967. Left to right: Rick Wright, Nick Mason, Syd Barrett, Roger Waters.

25

your own stoned fans in the hip city, and quite another
to play before a more conventional audience in the provinces just out for a few beers and a good time. Sometimes, the beer came pouring down from the balcony
onto the band.

It was, perhaps, the beginning of a realization that,
like most of its emerging San Francisco acid rock colleagues, Pink Floyd would prove an acquired taste to
the kinds of large audiences on which rock music
thrives. The music industry was in a transitional state in
1967, moving away from the promotional apparatus
that had worked in the past and toward a less well-defined career path for its artists. Pink Floyd was
caught in that transition in its early days as a professional band, and this caused significant problems for
them, not the least of which would be the departure of
their leading member.

And there wasn't much question, when Pink Floyd
entered Sound Techniques studio to cut their first
single (a catchy ditty than ran less than three minutes),
that its leading member was Syd Barrett. Barrett had
written the song in question, 'Arnold Layne,' an ode to a
transvestite, as well as its B-side, 'Candy and a Currant
Bun,' the re-titled version of their concert staple, 'Let's
Roll Another One.' (Note: Though it turned up in 1970
on *The Best of the Pink Floyd* in Holland and on *Masters
of Rock Vol. 1* in continental Europe in 1974, 'Candy
and a Currant Bun' has never been released on a US or
UK album.) Barrett had, in fact, written most of the
group's material, both the more conventional (if psychedelically arranged) pop songs to be used for singles
and some of its more experimental pieces. As far as the
band's managers and most of its fans were concerned,
Pink Floyd was Barrett and some backup musicians.

*Below:* Pink Floyd backstage at the Saville Theatre in London, 1 October 1967, shortly before their first promotional visit to America, during which Syd Barrett's behavior would precipitate his eventual departure from the group. Left to right: Rick Wright, Roger Waters, Nick Mason, Syd Barrett.

*Right:* An unusual publicity shot of Pink Floyd, taken in a junkyard.

*Right, below:* Syd Barrett, Pink Floyd's leader, gave the band its identity in its early years.

All of which seemed fine at the time, especially when two of the major record labels, Polydor and EMI, vied for the band on the basis of the single. EMI won the bidding war, and 'Arnold Layne'/'Candy and a Currant Bun' was released on 11 March 1967, on the label's Columbia imprint (not to be confused with the US Columbia label). 'Arnold Layne' entered the British charts on 30 March and reached Number 20. It was released in the US by EMI's subsidiary Capitol Records on the Tower label, but did not chart.

'Arnold Layne,' though a memorable pop song and very much in the eclectic style of its time, was not representative of what one was likely to hear at a Pink Floyd concert, and the band doesn't seem to have played it much, though they did appear on the popular *Top of the Pops* TV show to plug it. Meanwhile, they continued to play dates in London and around England during the spring, also going to EMI's Abbey Road studios to work on another single and their first album. The Beatles were in another room at the studios at the same time

*Below:* Pink Floyd's first two recordings: on the left, the cover of their US debut album, *Pink Floyd*; on the right, the soundtrack to *Tonite Let's All Make Love in London*.

working on *Sgt Pepper's Lonely Hearts Club Band*. Joe Boyd, as an independent producer, had been replaced by EMI staff producer Norman Smith.

Pink Floyd's second single, 'See Emily Play'/'Scarecrow' (both Barrett compositions), was released on 16 June. 'Emily' is one of the Floyd's and Barrett's best-remembered numbers. It was their biggest singles hit (and their last singles chart entry) for the next 12 years, going to Number 6.

The acquisition of an actual hit record, of course, meant that Pink Floyd had overcome a major hurdle in the progress of its career. But the achievement was also coincident (the degree to which it was causal is speculative) with problems in the behavior of Pink Floyd's leader, Syd Barrett. Producer Norman Smith has spoken of difficulties in dealing with Barrett in the studio, and such observers as Joe Boyd and David Gilmour relate encounters with Barrett around this time when he ignored them or seemed out of touch with

reality. There's no doubt Barrett was taking LSD during the period, but as his actions became more erratic, that didn't seem like an adequate explanation.

Of course, to stand out as odd in the pop world in the summer of 1967 took some doing, and these were only early signals that something was wrong. Pink Floyd continued to play around the country, sometimes even including their hit singles in their shows against their inclinations. On 5 August, the first Floyd album, *The Piper at the Gates of Dawn*, was released. (The title comes from a chapter in Kenneth Grahame's children's book *The Wind in the Willows*.) Eight of its 11 tracks were written by Barrett, with two group compositions and one by Waters. The album got to Number 6 in the British charts.

It is, of course, an album dominated by the work of Syd Barrett, and much of it has a nursery rhyme sound in both music and lyrics, though, especially in the band-composed instrumentals, 'Interstellar Overdrive' and

'Pow R Toc H,' the group rocks out convincingly. Nevertheless, the album owes its charm to Barrett's poetic, off-kilter words and unusual delivery, as well as to the surprising arrangements. The music obviously is influenced by that of such predecessors as the Beatles, but the influences also cross over. Listen to the Beatles' and the Rolling Stones' Christmas 1967 offerings, *Magical Mystery Tour* and *Their Satanic Majesties Request*, and you will hear sounds you heard earlier on *The Piper at the Gates of Dawn*.

Though this was the music that Pink Floyd's first listeners associated with the group, it is not, except for some of the instrumental passages and such elements as the occasional sound effect, similar to what they sounded like afterwards. It's impossible to know, but hard not to speculate, what the Pink Floyd sound would have been in later years had Syd Barrett remained in relative mental health and at the helm. Certainly, it would have been very different.

With the release of their first album, Pink Floyd added more TV appearances, interviews, photo sessions, and other promotional activities to their schedule, while still recording and playing concerts regularly. These activities continued into the fall, when Pink Floyd flew to the US for the first time for a promotional visit. Tower had released 'See Emily Play,' which reached Number 134, Pink Floyd's first US chart placing. In a procedure typical of the time, Tower also had cut three tracks from *The Piper at the Gates of Dawn*, added 'See Emily Play,' and released a nine-cut album called *Pink Floyd*.

The promotional trip, which Roger Waters would later call 'an amazing disaster,' began in San Francisco, logically enough, with Britain's own psychedelic band playing the Fillmore West for several nights. There were also a couple of TV appearances: A lipsynched performance of 'See Emily Play' on *American Bandstand* during which Barrett refused to mime, and one on Pat Boone's show that featured an interview in which Barrett refused to answer questions. The trip was cut short, and the band returned to England. (Despite this, *Pink Floyd* entered the US charts in December, getting to Number 131.)

Clearly, Barrett was not functioning adequately under the heavy workload of an up-and-coming band. The final straw seems to have been Pink Floyd's first formal UK tour, a package of acts headlined by the Jimi Hendrix Experience that opened at the Royal Albert Hall in London on 14 November and continued through 2 December, during which the group, third-billed, was

assigned a 17-minute set. It's fair to say that no one in the band was satisfied with the arrangement, and their dissatisfaction with various aspects of the way their career was being handled would manifest itself later, but Barrett's reaction was the least eloquent and the most extreme. He took to either not playing onstage or playing without regard to what the rest of the group was doing – that is, when he could be coaxed onstage at all.

In the midst of the tour, Pink Floyd released its third single, 'Apples and Oranges'/'Paint Box,' the B-side written by Rick Wright. It failed to chart, and Barrett's quoted reaction was that he couldn't care less. Like 'Candy and a Currant Bun,' 'Apples and Oranges' has never appeared on a US or UK album.

Pink Floyd is not the only group to have had a leading band member who was too unstable to engage in all the required activities of a pop band, and different groups have dealt with the problem in different ways. The Doors, for example, never went on a real tour, pre-

ferring isolated shows because they couldn't depend on lead singer Jim Morrison for extended periods of time. Pink Floyd at first seems to have tried the method adopted by the Beach Boys when their leader Brian Wilson suffered a nervous breakdown: They intended to replace him onstage but keep him for recordings. But Wilson, though the Beach Boys' writer/producer,

was not its sole lead singer, and even Wilson seems to have been somewhat more stable than Syd Barrett.

On 27 January 1968, it was announced that David Gilmour, Barrett's old friend from Cambridge, was joining Pink Floyd as second guitarist. On 2 March 1968, it was announced that Syd Barrett was no longer a member of Pink Floyd.

*Left:* Syd Barrett holds court
with Pink Floyd in San
Francisco in October 1967.

*Below:* Syd Barrett in 1970, a
year during which he released
two solo albums that marked
the end of his career as a
musician.

# Obscured by Clouds, 1968-73

Pink Floyd's dismissal of Syd Barrett has been second-guessed endlessly, not the least by the band members themselves. In fact, it is not a far stretch to interpret the overriding theme of such albums as *The Dark Side of the Moon* (which opens with the words, 'I've been mad for f***ing years'), *Wish You Were Here* (whose main song, 'Shine On You Crazy Diamond,' is explicitly about Barrett), and *The Wall* (the story of a crazed rock star, some of whose biographical details echo Waters's and some Barrett's) as an examination of what happened to Syd Barrett.

In the short term, however, it was other people who were questioning the decision. The group's singles had stopped charting and its concert fees had dropped,

*Left:* Syd Barrett, circa 1971, when he was well on his way to becoming the recluse that he remains today.

*Below:* David Gilmour at Pink Floyd's appearance at the Crystal Palace in London, 15 May 1971.

*Below:* Pink Floyd onstage in 1969, a year during which they toured extensively.

*Right:* Roger Waters in 1969 at a time when he was only beginning to assert himself as the band's de facto leader after the departure of Syd Barrett.

when they could get bookings. Jenner and King, who had always thought of Pink Floyd as Barrett's group, bailed out and stuck with him.

On 12 April, Pink Floyd released its fourth single, 'It Would Be So Nice'/'Julia Dream.' In the US, 'Julia Dream' was made the A-side. The single failed to chart in either country. (Once again, there's a lost song here: 'It Would Be So Nice' is not on any American or British album.)

At least with a more dependable lineup, it was possible to work more steadily. In May, the band recorded the soundtrack for a film called *The Committee* (no soundtrack album was released), and on 6 May, they launched a brief European tour. On 29 June, they released their second album, *A Saucerful of Secrets.* Only one of Barrett's compositions, 'Jugband Blues,' was used. Otherwise, the album was a showcase for what the new Pink Floyd could do, and it revealed the group straining to compose the kind of pop songs at which Barrett had excelled, but successfully pursuing extended, mostly instrumental songs such as Waters's 'Set the Controls for the Heart of the Sun' and the group composition 'A Saucerful of Secrets.' Reflecting the band's commercial decline (whether due to Barrett's absence or to the bad impression they'd given in person while he was still with them), the album did not match the success of the first LP, though it got to Number 9 in the UK. In the US, where a single of 'Remember a Day' was also released, the album did not chart.

The band's first American tour took place in July and

*Below:* Pink Floyd soundtrack albums, from left to right, *More, Obscured by Clouds*, and the UK and US editions of *Zabriskie Point*.

*Right, below:* Bulle Ogier encounters aboriginal life in *Obscured by Clouds* (also called *La Vallee* or *The Valley*).

*Far right:* Daria Halprin, co-star of Michelangelo Antonioni's *Zabriskie Point*.

*Right:* A scene from *More*, Barbet Schroeder's film-directing debut, which featured a soundtrack by Pink Floyd.

August, and was followed in September by a European tour. In October and November, Pink Floyd played selected British dates and recorded. The result of the latter activity was a fifth single, 'Point Me at the Sky'/ 'Careful With That Axe, Eugene,' which again did not chart. It was the last single Pink Floyd would release for 11 years. (And 'Point Me at the Sky' became another non-LP single rarity.)

The first half of 1969 found Pink Floyd touring Britain, notably playing a show called 'More Furious Madness from the Massed Gadgets of Auximenes' at the Royal Festival Hall in London, which, with a sea monster in the aisle and a quadrophonic sound system featuring speakers in the back of the room, is remembered as the first of Pink Floyd's elaborate stage shows.

At dates in Birmingham and Manchester, the band recorded the shows for a live album, but the next LP release was their first full movie soundtrack to appear on record, *More*, which came out in July. Pink Floyd's two soundtrack albums (the other is *Obscured by Clouds*, like *More* used in a film directed by Barbet Schroeder) are much better than one might assume from the genre in general or from the amount of time the band spent making them. In fact, *More* contains several excellent Waters songs, notably 'Cirrus Minor,' 'The Nile Song,' and 'Cymbaline,' and the last even made it into Pink Floyd's set list for a time. Further, the soundtracks allowed Pink Floyd to work out ideas without being judged as harshly as they would be for a 'regular' Pink Floyd album. And it was already apparent that the band members would need time to develop their own style after having been thrust into the creative end of the music by the loss of Syd Barrett. *More* also sold reasonably well, hitting Number 9 in the UK.

Three months later came the live album, *Ummagumma*, a double-record set that featured a bonus album on which each band member was given half a side to pursue a solo experiment. The experi-

ments had varying success, but the live record, which contained four extended pieces, each running 8 to 12 minutes, finally put on vinyl an accurate portrayal of the aural part of a Pink Floyd concert.

As a result, *Ummagumma* became Pink Floyd's most successful album to date. It reached Number 5 in the UK and even scored in the US, where it got to Number 74, only the band's second album to chart there.

January 1970 marked the LP release of the next Pink Floyd effort in a movie, the soundtrack of Michelangelo Antonioni's *Zabriskie Point*. Though the band had recorded an entire score for the film, Antonioni opted to use only two pieces of Floyd music, one for the film's opening credits and another for its cataclysmic finale. Not surprisingly, it is that ending that most people remember as the film's high point.

The month also saw the release of Syd Barrett's first solo album, *The Madcap Laughs*. Produced partially by Malcolm Jones (who gave up) and partially by David

Gilmour and Roger Waters, the album features some fascinating songs, though it sounds as though Barrett simply played demos on acoustic guitar, to which other instruments were in some cases overdubbed. Barrett would try again, with the album *Barrett*, released in November 1970, and would even take another abortive shot at recording in 1974, but the evidence of the recordings, if not the songs, seems to support the notion that Barrett would not have been able to function in Pink Floyd had he stayed. In the early 1970s, he moved back to Cambridge and, except for a couple of live appearances, was not involved in the music business again.

Pink Floyd maintained a busy schedule in 1970, touring Britain in the first quarter of the year and the US in May. On 27 June, they premiered a new extended piece, 'Atom Heart Mother,' at the Bath Festival. It became Pink Floyd's policy (at least up until the mid-1970s) to play much of its major work in concert

*Below:* Syd Barrett at the shoot for the cover of his debut solo album, *The Madcap Laughs.* Released in the UK in January 1970, it didn't see US release until 1974, in a double package with his second album, *Barrett.*

*before* recording it, a far different approach from that of most performers and one that made different demands on their audiences, admitting them into the creative process and sometimes requiring their patience. Pink Floyd continued to play 'Atom Heart Mother' on a European tour in June and July, at a free concert in Hyde Park in London on 18 July, and during a US tour in September and October.

*Atom Heart Mother*, Pink Floyd's first group studio album to be released without the participation of Syd Barrett, was released in Great Britain on 10 October 1970. Even those who had heard the title composition in concert were in for a surprise, since the group had turned to composer Ron Geesin to overdub an orchestra and choir onto the piece. Geesin had been working on a soundtrack album with Roger Waters (*The Body*, released toward the end of the year), and this had led to his collaboration with the band as a whole. 'Atom Heart Mother' certainly made the case for Pink Floyd music in an orchestral context and showed them developing an ability to construct long works, not just to improvise over a given pattern. The album was also a hit, topping the British charts and reaching a new peak of Number 55 in America.

Encouraged, the band spent large parts of the first several months of 1971 in the recording studio trying to top *Atom Heart Mother*. They also got in several British dates and took off for a European tour in June. In August, they toured the Far East for the first time, and there were more British and European dates (and more recording sessions) throughout the summer. Meanwhile, impatient for a new album, EMI released *Relics*, a collection of non-LP singles and other odd tracks, in May 1971. A North American tour ran from mid-October to 20 November, during which time *Meddle*, the album they had been working on for so long, was released.

Like *Atom Heart Mother, Meddle* was an album that featured one side-long composition, 'Echoes,' and several shorter pieces on the other side. There was no orchestra this time, but the group had clearly found a way to make long instrumental works consistently interesting, inserting tempo changes and new musical passages in such a way as to keep the listener engaged. If anything was missing, it was a true lyrical focus, though certainly by this point Pink Floyd's listeners were not looking to it for the kinds of songs

*Left:* David Gilmour onstage in the early 1970s, at a time when his guitar playing and singing were coming to represent the sound of Pink Floyd.

*Below:* Roger Waters, who, as the early 1970s passed, took over all the lyric-writing and much of the composing for Pink Floyd.

80th ANNIVERSARY SEASON

*Monday Evening May 1, 1972, and Tuesday Evening May 2, 1972, at 8:00*

Ron Delsener presents

# Pink Floyd

David Gilmour          Nick Mason

Roger Waters         Richard Wright

Syd Barrett had provided, or that other groups did. Pink Floyd had carved their own niche, one that, in the UK anyway, was large enough to allow them into the upper reaches of the charts. *Meddle* got to Number 3 and stayed in the charts longer than any previous Pink Floyd album. This was also true in America, although the album only made it to Number 70.

The band felt that its US record company, Capitol, was responsible for its relatively low chart placings, and went looking for a replacement, eventually settling on the Columbia Records division of CBS Records.

Though they had signed (for a hefty advance) to the label, for the US only, by the end of 1972, they still owed their next regular studio release to Capitol. Their first Columbia album, in fact, would not be released until 1975. (In Britain, however, the band continued to record for EMI.)

Pink Floyd began 1972 with a British tour, and, during a four-day stand at the Rainbow Theatre in London, they premiered their next extended piece, 'The Dark Side of the Moon' (sometimes also called 'Eclipse'). It would be a full year before an album by that

title was released. March found the band back in Japan, and in April and May they toured America. June marked the release of the band's second Barbet Schroeder film soundtrack, *Obscured by Clouds*, which again makes instructional listening in the group's development. Listen, for example, to Waters's 'Free Four,' a straightforward song with lyrics about life, death, and touring, very much the work of the man who would write the lyrics to Pink Floyd's major albums to come.

September found Pink Floyd back on tour in the US, playing 'The Dark Side of the Moon' at every show, and in October they were back in the studio recording it. *Pink Floyd Live at Pompeii*, a film featuring the band playing in an empty amphitheater and working in the studio, had its premiere, though it was not widely shown until years later. The band toured Europe in November and December, then returned to the studio in January, finishing *The Dark Side of the Moon* on 1 February. Released a month later, the album would be a turning point for the band.

# The Dark Side of the Moon, 1973-82

During the five years between the departure of Syd Barrett and the release of *The Dark Side of the Moon*, the members of Pink Floyd lived the busy lives of moderately successful rock musicians. When they weren't touring, they were recording — that is, if they weren't writing new material, working on their stage show, or doing interviews. The task of sustaining themselves and even increasing their popularity was hobbled by their disinclination (or apparent inability) to write songs that fit sufficiently into radio formats to become hit singles, and due to the lack of a visual or vocal focus in the group. The latter could partially be ascribed to a fear of putting anyone out front after the damage the band suffered when Barrett proved unable to handle the job of frontman, and partly to the times. The popular music of the late 1960s and early 1970s saw rock breaking away from the kind of mass success enjoyed by the Beatles and appealing to a more specific, albeit extremely large audience that wasn't interested in the trappings of pop. To them, the band's

anonymous, blue-jeaned image was just the right one for a hip rock group.

Gradually, through that cycle of touring and recording, Pink Floyd was building an audience of its own, especially in the US and in Europe – an audience attuned to its lengthy compositions and to stage shows that emphasized lighting effects, films, and a surrounding sound system rather than what the band looked like. In fact, with only a couple of album covers even showing their faces, the band members did not enjoy (or suffer) the recognition most public figures experience. Amazingly, this remained true even after the release of *The Dark Side of the Moon*.

Based on the following Pink Floyd had amassed by the start of 1973, it would have been easy to predict that their next album would do better than its predecessors, and might even break them out to the mass success that had so far eluded them in the US. And certainly, *The Dark Side of the Moon*, which featured more songs of shorter lengths than had been typical for a Pink Floyd album (even if they were linked together into a single piece) – songs with identifiable melodies and lyrics – was arguably the most accessible album they had made since *The Piper at the Gates of Dawn*. Still, there is no explaining the success the album achieved.

For the record, *The Dark Side of the Moon* was an out-of-the-box hit. It entered the American charts on 17 March and hit Number 1 six weeks later, by which time it had become Pink Floyd's first gold album (indicating sales of 500,000 copies). It entered the British charts on 31 March and peaked at Number 2. All that is remarkable enough, especially in America, where Pink Floyd had never gotten above Number 55, but the more amazing, inexplicable part is how long *The Dark Side of the Moon* continued to sell. In England, it stayed in the charts for 294 weeks – more than five years – a total exceeded by only five other albums in history. In America, it spent 741 weeks – more than 14 years – in

the charts, by far the longest any album sold well enough to be listed. *The Dark Side of the Moon* has been certified for sales of 12 million copies in the US, making it the fourth best-selling album of all time, and it is estimated to have sold another 13 million in the rest of the world.

Of course, the main way that *The Dark Side of the Moon* differed from other Pink Floyd albums was that it presented a set of philosophical lyrics, all penned by Roger Waters. In deceptively simple words, Waters explored fundamental issues of life: work, the passage of time, money, war, madness, and death. These reflections were sung over frequently calm music dominated by electronic keyboard patterns and complemented by forceful guitar solos, all of it punctuated by various carefully arranged sound effects – chiming clocks, ringing cash registers, a heartbeat, etc.

Much of this was not new to Pink Floyd; in fact, such tunes as 'Breathe' (originally on Waters's and Geesin's soundtrack to *The Body*) and 'Us and Them' (written for, but not used in, *Zabriskie Point*) had been in the band's repertoire for several years. But *The Dark Side of the Moon* represented both a culmination of the aural experiments Pink Floyd had been making for the previous five years and the flowering of Waters's lyrical facility. The result was a piece of music that defined an era and continues to be heard frequently 20 years later.

The album's overwhelming success vaulted Pink Floyd from the ranks of middle-level rock bands to the upper reaches of their profession, and led to enormous changes in their career. This did not occur immediately. The day that *The Dark Side of the Moon* entered the US charts in March, Pink Floyd was playing a midnight

*Above:* Roger Waters, who, with the success of *The Dark Side of the Moon*, took on the responsibility of writing the bulk of Pink Floyd's material.

*Right:* The 40-foot circular screen became a trademark of Pink Floyd in concert after *The Dark Side of the Moon*'s success. A variety of illustrations and lighting effects appeared on the screen throughout the shows.

*Above:* Smoke created by dry ice was a favorite Pink Floyd stage effect in the early-mid 1970s.

*Left:* An eyeball is projected on the screen, framed by streaks of light, during a mid-1975 performance.

*Below:* Examples of Pink Floyd album art (most of it by the firm of Hipgnosis) from the 1970s: the brick cover of *The Wall*, the prism design of *The Dark Side of the Moon*, the handshake cover photo of *Wish You Were Here* (originally hidden under a wrapping), and the pig floating over Battersea Power Station on the cover of *Animals*.

*Below:* Backup singers (at left) join Pink Floyd on stage as the screen becomes the dark side of the moon.

show at the 5000-seat Radio City Music Hall in New York City, part of a tour of theater-size venues. When they returned to the US for more touring in mid-June, they would open at Roosevelt Stadium in Jersey City, New Jersey, and thereafter their concerts would be held in arenas seating upwards of 10,000 or in outdoor stadiums that might allow for five or even ten times that number.

After a summer break, the band returned to the recording studio in October 1973, with the ambitious intention of creating an album without the use of musical instruments. Wine bottles, rubber bands, aerosol cans, and adhesive tape were all mentioned as sources for sound on the album, to be called *Household Objects*. This project, however, was abandoned.

The ongoing success of *The Dark Side of the Moon* and the switch of record labels in the US eased the usual demand for a yearly album, and the group spent the first half of 1974 working on separate projects. Waters wrote new Pink Floyd material, while Mason and Gilmour took on outside production jobs, Mason

producing former Soft Machine member Robert Wyatt's album *Rock Bottom*, while Gilmour handled Unicorn's *Blue Pine Trees*.

In the absence of new music, and with Pink Floyd more commercial than ever, EMI reissued the group's first two albums as *A Nice Pair* and saw the package hit the charts in both the US and the UK.

Pink Floyd returned to action in mid-1974 for a short tour of France, during which they performed material from *The Dark Side of the Moon* and introduced a new set of songs including 'Shine On You Crazy Diamond,' 'Raving and Drooling,' and 'Gotta Be Crazy.' This was a dry run for a British tour that began in November. In order to make the desired impression in the larger venues now being played, Pink Floyd added to its stage set a 40-foot circular screen that would become a trademark of its shows, on which a variety of lighting effects, photographs, and films were displayed.

In January 1975, Pink Floyd began recording its next album. The sessions lasted into March, then were interrupted by a tour of the West Coast of North America.

Sessions continued in May and June. On the last day before the group would again break for an American East Coast tour, Syd Barrett, overweight and with a shaven head and eyebrows, turned up at the studio and announced that he was ready to rejoin the band, an offer that seems not to have been taken seriously. The irony, of course, could not have been greater: Pink Floyd was working on the new album's primary song,

'Shine On You Crazy Diamond,' which was about Barrett, and the album itself would be titled *Wish You Were Here*.

The album was premiered, with technical difficulty, at Pink Floyd's Knebworth concert on 5 July, and finished in recording sessions later in the month. It was released on 15 September.

For those who had heard Pink Floyd's concert per-

formances of 1974-75, *Wish You Were Here* was something of a surprise in that it did not contain 'Raving and Drooling' or 'Gotta Be Crazy.' 'Shine On You Crazy Diamond' was presented in two parts that opened and closed the album, its extended, bluesy instrumental parts giving way to lyrics that paid tribute to a 'piper' who was 'caught in the cross fire of childhood and stardom.' The two sections of the song were broken up by three new songs. 'Welcome to the Machine' and especially 'Have a Cigar' (sung by Roy Harper) had arch, cynical lyrics relating to the music business, while 'Wish You Were Here' also spoke bitterly about compromises made in life. The music, though compelling, echoed the album's themes. *Wish You Were Here* moved from the philosophical, sometimes sad tone of *The Dark Side of the Moon* to scathing sarcasm.

Pink Floyd did not tour behind the album, which may have reduced its commercial impact, though its sales were not shabby. It hit Number 1 in both the US and the UK, and has sold approximately 10 million copies worldwide.

The group retreated from the public eye for the remainder of 1975 and all of 1976, only garnering headlines in December of 1976, when a photo shoot for the next album cover went awry and a giant, inflated pig came loose from its moorings above the Battersea Power Plant and went flying off over the British countryside. The pig, which would join Pink Floyd's list of stage props, nevertheless graced the cover of *Animals* when it was released on 23 January 1977.

*Animals* contained the earlier Pink Floyd songs 'Gotta Be Crazy' (renamed 'Dogs') and 'Raving and Drooling' (renamed 'Sheep') in a thematic album that echoed George Orwell's novella *Animal Farm*, dividing the world up into types of people identified with pigs, dogs, and sheep. The album's pessimism was

Bottom: Roger Waters
onstage in 1977, singing a
portion of his latest opus,
*Animals*, while wearing
headphones to make sure
he's in sync with the other
musicians and the various
visual effects.

leavened by its prologue and coda, 'Pigs on the Wing,' which spoke out for human compassion. Once again, Roger Waters had taken on large lyrical concerns, and this time he had also composed much of the music. Only 'Dogs' carried a co-writing credit, to David Gilmour.

The album did not match the massive commercial success of its predecessors, getting to Number 2 in the UK and Number 3 in the US and staying in the charts only through the summer of 1977. It has sold approximately six million copies worldwide.

The drop in sales came despite a six-month tour — the last major tour ever undertaken by this version of Pink Floyd — dubbed 'Pink Floyd: In the Flesh' that covered Europe and North America and played mostly in stadiums. By the end of the tour, Waters had become extremely disenchanted with such giant shows, which he felt simply put the audience at too much of a distance from the band. His feelings would be expressed in his next writings for Pink Floyd.

After the tour ended in July, Pink Floyd dispersed temporarily. Waters went home to write, Gilmour and

Wright began work on solo albums, and Mason went back to record producing, surprisingly working with the punk band the Damned on their album *For Your Pleasure* and, more typically, co-producing Soft Machine guitarist Steve Hillage's *Green*.

Gilmour's solo album, *David Gilmour*, was released on 25 May 1978, followed shortly thereafter by Rick Wright's *Wet Dream*. Wright's jazzy album, largely consisting of instrumental music, disappeared quickly. Gilmour's more conventional pop-rock collection, recorded with members of his pre-Pink Floyd group Jokers Wild, reached Number 17 in the UK and Number 29 in the US, healthy sales considering the lack of name recognition for a member of Pink Floyd, especially without much in the way of promotional work, but still no competition to the group itself.

Waters returned to Pink Floyd with two proposals for another concept album for the group. One was called *The Wall* and concerned the life of a rock star for whom

a psychological barrier between himself and the world grows up due to his unhappy life experiences. The other was a series of dreams entitled *The Pros and Cons of Hitch Hiking*. The band chose *The Wall*.

*The Wall*, which eventually took up two records when it was released on 30 November 1979, was the most ambitious project ever undertaken by Roger Waters or Pink Floyd. In the annals of rock theme albums or 'operas,' it was perhaps the most daring and, for the same reason, the most indulgent – for *The Wall* was, in fact, an extended reflection on the travails of a rock star who very closely resembled Roger Waters.

Like Waters, 'Pink Floyd,' the name given *The Wall*'s major character, loses his father as an infant. He has trouble with school and suffers from a smothering mother. When he becomes a rock star, he's forced to tour extensively, which he finds disorienting and which leads to a breakup with his wife. All of these experiences serve as bricks in the wall surrounding him,

*Right:* One of the giant puppets designed by Gerald Scarfe for use in the stage version of *The Wall*, which played only a few week-long engagements in selected cities in 1980 and 1981.

*Left:* Intermission at a performance of *The Wall* at the Nassau Coliseum in New York, 25 February 1980. At the end of the first act, the wall is completely constructed, blocking the audience's view of the band.

*Below:* Gerald Scarfe's swastika-like symbols presage the fascist rally sequence in *The Wall*, as Roger Waters, playing the part of Pink, sits onstage, about to become 'Comfortably Numb.'

such that, by the end of the album's first record, he is completely walled in. In his hotel room on tour, he fantasizes about war, and after he has been given an injection to get him ready to perform, he transforms his concert into a fascist rally. When he finally decides to quit, he fantasizes a trial in which his various tormentors testify and he is found guilty of 'showing feelings,' only to have the judge rule that the wall must be torn down.

Though the other members of Pink Floyd considered this story more universal than the scattered *Hitch Hiking*, it may not sound like the perfect prescription for a hit album. Especially by comparing rock concerts to fascist rallies, Waters was turning on its head a basic assumption about rock music – that it unifies a mass audience in some sort of humanistic way. Maybe that *was* always a fantasy, but could rock fans actually be expected to spend money and time listening to Waters dispel it?

*The Wall*, as it turned out, came second only to *The Dark Side of the Moon* among Pink Floyd's most successful albums. 'Another Brick in the Wall, Part Two,' released as a single in advance of the album, topped

*Bottom:* Bob Geldof, in the posture he is most frequently seen adopting in *Pink Floyd The Wall*, playing the part of the catatonic rock star 'Pink Floyd.'

the charts on both sides of the Atlantic, and the album stayed at Number 1 in the US for 15 weeks (it hit Number 3 in Britain), eventually selling eight million copies. Worldwide, it has sold another nine million.

Though a promotional tour, which would be Pink Floyd's first since 1977, seemed inevitable, Waters was conscious that the very theme of *The Wall* mitigated against it. How could one perform a piece so critical of mass concerts at mass concerts? The dilemma was solved by staging weeklong presentations of *The Wall* in Los Angeles and New York in February 1980, and in London in August. (It was staged a fourth time in Germany in February 1981.) Even then, the shows were unusual to say the least, calling for the building of a wall between the band and the audience such that, for much of the second half of the show, the band was not visible. Some observers were impressed; others left early.

Nevertheless, the visual potential of the project was

obvious, and the band set to work turning *The Wall* into a film, a project that would take a considerable amount of time and go through several permutations in the course of a couple of years. In June 1981, for example, Pink Floyd again played a series of performances of *The Wall* in London for the purpose of filming them to use in the movie. But none of this footage turned up in the final film.

Meanwhile, drummer Nick Mason released a solo album in 1981 called *Nick Mason's Fictitious Sports*. It was actually an album by New York avant-garde jazz composer Carla Bley on which Mason served as drummer and to which he lent his name and connection to a major label. In November 1981, EMI and Columbia released a Pink Floyd compilation ironically titled *A Collection of Great Dance Songs*.

The band, especially Roger Waters, continued to work on the film of *The Wall*, bringing in director Alan Parker, who finally put the production in motion, hiring

Boomtown Rats singer Bob Geldof to play Pink. The result, titled *Pink Floyd The Wall*, premiered on 14 July 1982. Nearly without dialogue, the film was in essence a full-length music video of the album, combining live action with the surreal animation of Gerald Scarfe. It garnered mixed reviews, but was a financial success.

On 26 July, Pink Floyd's record labels issued the band's first new music in two and a half years, a single called 'When the Tigers Broke Free'/'Bring the Boys Back Home,' with a notation saying that the A-side was 'taken from the album *The Final Cut*.' The single, both of whose songs appeared in the movie, reached Number 39 in the UK but did not chart in America.

*The Final Cut*, originally intended to be an album of extra music either from outtakes or added film music from *The Wall*, turned into something entirely different when it was released almost a year later. By then, its title had taken on a very different meaning.

# The Final Cut, 1983-92

Although the release of *The Final Cut*, the last Pink Floyd album to credit both Roger Waters and David Gilmour, marked the culmination of several trends that had been progressing in the band for 10 years, the record nevertheless came as something of a surprise to fans. For one thing, the album, for the first time on a Pink Floyd LP since *Meddle*, listed the personnel of the band, and it had changed. Pink Floyd was now a trio consisting of Waters, Gilmour, and Mason.

It later came out that keyboard player Rick Wright had been bought out of the Pink Floyd partnership prior to the release of *The Wall*, reportedly due to Waters's dissatisfaction with him, though all agreed to the change, and then had been hired to play at *The Wall* concerts in 1980 and 1981, to give the appearance that the group was still intact.

That wasn't all one could learn simply by reading the credits on the back cover of *The Final Cut*. The album was subtitled 'a requiem for the post war dream,' 'by Roger Waters,' 'performed by Pink Floyd.' Waters, in

other words, was now billed above the band, which was augmented by five other musicians and the National Philharmonic Orchestra. The album was dedicated to Waters's father, and its cover was designed not by the firm of Hipgnosis, which had done most of the Pink Floyd album covers, but by the ubiquitous Roger Waters.

The dominant sound on the album, which had become a loose concept record treating war and international politics, was Waters's voice, pitched in the strained upper register he had frequently employed on *The Wall*. Gilmour turned up singing only the verses of 'Not Now John,' the album's closest thing to a rocker and far and away the best song on the record. (Released as a single, it got to Number 30 in the UK.) It is no wonder that many Pink Floyd fans considered *The Final Cut* a Roger Waters solo album in everything but name.

But, as would become more and more obvious during the 1980s with regard to Pink Floyd, there actually is a great deal in a name. *The Final Cut*, while it

*Left:* The new Pink Floyd in 1990, at the time of the Knebworth concert. Left to right: Rick Wright, Dave Gilmour, and Nick Mason.

*Right:* David Gilmour at a radio station, giving one of the many interviews he began granting in the mid-1980s, after the Pink Floyd split.

*Right, below:* Nick Mason, whose loyalty seemed to shift from Waters to Gilmour, as plans for a new Pink Floyd shaped up.

didn't sell as well as other Pink Floyd albums released after *The Dark Side of the Moon*, did sell. It was certified for sales of a million copies in the US, where it reached Number 6, and it got to Number 1 in the UK, where its antiwar statements were taken, correctly, as Waters's reaction to the 1982 Falklands conflict.

The album might have done better if, as planned, Pink Floyd had gone on tour to promote it. But those plans were shelved, and both Waters and Gilmour set to work on solo albums.

When considering a group that never saw fit to tell anyone it had fired its keyboard player, setting a date for the 'breakup' of Pink Floyd – even if we decide to call it that – isn't easy. As early as September 1982, Roger Waters was telling *Rolling Stone* in essence that *he* was Pink Floyd and that he didn't feel the need to pretend otherwise anymore. The band's future, he said, 'depends very much on me.' In a September 1988 article in *Penthouse* magazine that presents Waters's side of the story, music journalist Timothy White flatly states, 'The Floyd broke up in 1983 – notwithstanding all flamboyant appearances to the contrary.'

But as the late Nicholas Shaffner wrote in his 1991 biography, *Saucerful of Secrets: The Pink Floyd Story*, which, though seeking more of a balance, essentially presents Gilmour's side of the story, the guitarist 'now insists that he ''always made it absolutely clear to Roger'' that ''If you go, man, we're carrying on.'' '

This seems at least slightly at odds with Gilmour's actions. His second solo album, *About Face*, recorded

between July and October of 1983, is very different from 1978's *David Gilmour*, which he was now saying he had recorded 'for fun.' Co-produced by Bob Ezrin, who had worked on *The Wall*, the album featured such ace musicians as drummer Jeff Porcaro (of Toto and perhaps the most in-demand session drummer since Hal Blaine until his death in 1992) and Steve Winwood. Two of its songs were co-written by Pete Townshend.

In interviews (the first given by anyone in the band since the early 1970s), Gilmour was ambivalent about the group's future. 'Given the situation that I can't really rely on the others in Pink Floyd to come and work whenever I want them to,' he told Kevin Hennessy of *Music Sound Output*, 'it was necessary to do that [i.e., put a lot of effort into *About Face*] in order to make a good record which would serve me in my ongoing career.'

David Gilmour's ongoing career – under the name David Gilmour – was set in motion by the release of *About Face* on 5 March 1984 and the launch of a tour of Europe and North America that began on 31 March in Dublin. The tour ran through 16 July, a lengthy trek that was more successful in the US than it was in Europe, where ticket sales sometimes failed to break the 1000 mark for a show. The album got to Number 21 in the UK and Number 32 in the US.

Roger Waters, for his part, had returned to his other 1978 writing project, *The Pros and Cons of Hitch Hiking*. Employing many of the same musicians he had added for *The Final Cut*, Waters solved the problem of replacing Gilmour's distinctive guitar sound by persuading Eric Clapton to play on the album.

*Left:* David Gilmour ponders his future in the mid-1980s.

*Left, bottom:* A publicity photo taken in 1984 for David Gilmour's solo album and tour. Soon enough, he decided to take a different approach.

*Below:* Promotional materials for Roger Waters and David Gilmour solo projects such as *The Pros and Cons of Hitch Hiking, Radio K.A.O.S.,* and *About Face.*

*Overleaf:* Two views of David Gilmour as he appeared in November 1984 at a concert billed with nine other guitarists as 'Guitar Greats' at the Capitol Theater in Passaic, New Jersey, which was staged and filmed by MTV. Gilmour undertook a number of side projects in the mid-1980s before settling on the idea of going on under the Pink Floyd banner.

Unfortunately, the LP ended up justifying Pink Floyd's decision not to be involved with it. *Pros and Cons*, much of which seemed sexist (along with its tacky cover), was hard to follow despite extensive lyrics and difficult to listen to because of a lack of melody. Even Waters defender Kurt Loder, reviewing it in *Rolling Stone*, called *Pros and Cons* a 'faintly hideous record.' Though the presence of Clapton as a sideman enabled Waters to play arenas in his North American tour, which ran through July and August, then returned, sans Clapton, in March and April 1985, the album, released on 8 May 1984, only hit Number 31 in the US. It got to Number 13 in the UK.

Other current or former Pink Floyd members were also active, if less so: Rick Wright, in a duo with Dave Harris called Zee, released the album *Identity* in 1984; Nick Mason released an album called *Profiles* in 1985 with Rick Fenn.

One of the guest musicians on *Profiles* was David Gilmour, who sang the album's single, 'Lie for a Lie.' His participation on the record can, in retrospect, be taken as an interesting signal of his possible intention to work with Mason, whose best friend in Pink Floyd had always been Waters, but also as typical of Gilmour's activities in the year after his fling with a solo career.

Indeed, Gilmour seems to be on nearly every rock record that came out of Britain in late 1984 and 1985, from LPs by Paul McCartney, Pete Townshend, and Bryan Ferry to less likely names such as Grace Jones and the Duran Duran offshoot Arcadia. Gilmour also found another protégé (he had been an important booster of the career of Kate Bush in the 1970s) in the Beatlesque Dream Academy and co-produced their debut album.

A hint of what Gilmour might do next was given in *Juke* magazine in November 1985, when Mason was

interviewed and said of Pink Floyd, '[W]e definitely haven't agreed that it's all over. I think that things have changed because David and myself are interested in revitalizing it, whereas two years ago nobody was.'

Waters, meanwhile, was less interested than ever. He had taken on a new manager in June 1985, and sought to sever the duties of Pink Floyd's manager, Steve O'Rourke, even going so far as to offer Gilmour and Mason the rights to the band's name if they'd join him in dumping O'Rourke. When they refused, Waters, in December 1985, officially left Pink Floyd, asking EMI and Columbia to release him from his contractual obli-

gations since he was no longer a member of the group.

In 1986, Waters worked on the soundtrack for the film *When the Wind Blows*, a post-nuclear-holocaust animated movie that appeared in October. Then, on Halloween, 20 years to the day after Pink Floyd had signed its first management agreement, Waters filed suit to have the name Pink Floyd retired. By this time, it had become obvious that Gilmour and Mason intended to make an album as Pink Floyd – they had even hired producer Bob Ezrin, who had pulled out of an agreement to produce Waters's next album.

This was confirmed on 11 November 1986, when

*Left:* Roger Waters's 1984 touring band included Eric Clapton, who is pictured here second from left.

*Left, below:* The Roger Waters 1984 band at work. The drummer is Andy Newmark.

*Below:* The male animated character in *When the Wind Blows*, a film with soundtrack by Roger Waters that follows two ordinary people who survive nuclear war, only to fall victim to the fallout. Don't rent it for the kiddies.

'Pink Floyd' issued a statement to the effect that 'the group have no intention of disbanding. On the contrary, David Gilmour and Nick Mason with Rick Wright [who had been hired again] and producer Bob Ezrin, are currently recording a new album.' The battle lines were thus drawn.

That Roger Waters was not winning the legal battle seemed confirmed in the spring of 1987 when, at the conclusion of a press release announcing the upcoming release of Waters's new album, *Radio K.A.O.S.*, came these words: '[A]ttorneys on behalf of Roger Waters today issued the following statement: "Pink Floyd recorded a number of highly successful albums between 1967 and 1983, including 'Dark Side of the Moon' and 'The Wall'. Roger Waters was the major songwriter and producer of the albums as well as the lead singer and creative force. The dispute with the other members of Pink Floyd is proceeding in the courts to resolve the question of rights to the name and assets of Pink Floyd, which include the many stage effects used in the past. This litigation will probably not be resolved until 1988 at the earliest. Despite press reports to the contrary, Waters has not dropped any of his claims. Waters will not again record or perform with Dave Gilmour and Nick Mason under the name of Pink Floyd or at all."'

That Waters found it necessary to deny that the battle was over and that he was rejoining Pink Floyd was evidence enough that things weren't going well for him, but perhaps more significant was the reference to 'rights to the name and assets of Pink Floyd,' which indicated that the tenor of the dispute had moved from Waters's contention that Pink Floyd did not exist (and could not, therefore, issue new albums or go on tour) to

*Below:* Roger Waters, as he appeared in 1990 around the time of the benefit performance of *The Wall* in Berlin.

*Right:* David Gilmour recording with Queen guitarist Brian May.

*Left, below:* Pink Floyd-related live recordings, 1990's *The Wall Live in Berlin*, by Roger Waters, and 1989's *Delicate Sound of Thunder*, by David Gilmour's version of Pink Floyd.

*Right:* Pink Floyd albums of the 1980s, with and without Roger Waters.

a dispute about how to divide the spoils in what was now a sort of divorce case. The terms of that divorce might not have been agreed to yet, but Gilmour and Mason were going to have the chance to present their case to a jury of Pink Floyd fans both on record and in person.

Waters, meanwhile, had put together a far more tuneful effort in *Radio K.A.O.S.*, even if the album's storyline, which has a paraplegic computer genius staging a mock nuclear holocaust in order to scare the world into disarmament, was pretentious and un-wieldy. On a North American tour that started on 15 August, Waters proved an engaging frontman, his show including early Pink Floyd videos shown on the in-evitable circular screen and a DJ booth in the center of the auditorium. The tour's first leg ran through 29 September. Unfortunately, the public responded dis-appointingly to the album, which reached Number 50 in the US, and Number 25 in the UK.

Gilmour, for his part, seems to have had some trouble putting together a Pink Floyd album by himself, even suffering the indignity of a meeting with Ezrin and a representative of CBS at which he was told his work so far was not Floydian enough. The result was an album that credited 16 musicians in addition to Gilmour, Mason, and Wright, plus six writers other than Gilmour, all trying to make the album 'sound like Pink Floyd.' (Shaffner dismisses this army by saying that Gilmour is generous about giving credit to others.)

The irony here is considerable since, if there was any constant in Pink Floyd's music from 1967 to 1983, it was change. Such musical development was typical of bands of the 1960s – when the Beatles produced *Sgt Pepper's Lonely Hearts Club Band*, nobody said that it wasn't them because it didn't sound like 'I Want to Hold Your Hand.' *The Piper at the Gates of Dawn* doesn't really sound like *The Dark Side of the Moon*, and neither

sound like *The Wall*. So what does it mean to sound like Pink Floyd?

Listening to *A Momentary Lapse of Reason*, the album that resulted from the effort, it seems that slow tempos, sound effects of various kinds, and vague lyrics touching on such topics as movies, flying, and machinery, in addition to the guitar work and singing of David Gilmour, are the ingredients. Add in a typically surreal Hipgnosis album cover and a massive world tour featuring many of the 'stage effects used in the past,' and you have the Pink Floyd of 1987-90.

This edition of Pink Floyd met with massive success. *A Momentary Lapse of Reason*, released on 7 September 1987, hit Number 3 in the US and in the UK, and its world sales eventually reached six million copies. The tour kicked off on 9 September and played across North America through December, moving on to the Far East in January 1988. By spring, it was in Europe, and in the summer it was back in the US. It continued on into 1989, and didn't finish up until Knebworth, on 30 June 1990.

By that time, an agreement of sorts had been reached with Waters, such that, for example, he re-tained rights to stage *The Wall* and to be credited for such 'stage effects' as the pig (Gilmour and Mason had even tried changing the pig's sex to avoid infringement, but in the end were forced to acknowledge Waters in the credits to their tour video and album, *Delicate Sound of Thunder*, released in 1989). The exact terms were not made public, but a sense of Waters's frustra-tion can be gleaned from his 2 February 1988 interview remark, '[T]he only case that the law is interested in me bringing is one saying, "Well, if you go on calling your-self Pink Floyd I demand that you pay me 20 or 25 per-cent of the cake." I'm not interested in the cake! So I don't think there's very much that I can do.'

Despite Waters's declaration that 'it shouldn't just be

a kind of franchise,' the rock world had long since bowed to business realities regarding brand names, and there were bands (one thinks of Yes and Fleetwood Mac for starters) with far greater continuity problems than the current legally verified Pink Floyd who continued to record and to tour.

The moral question is stickier. Is Pink Floyd Syd Barrett's group, and did it cease to exist in 1968? Or is Pink Floyd the quartet that made its most popular album, *The Dark Side of the Moon*, with Roger Waters writing lyrics and all four members collaborating on music? Is it the Waters-dominated group of the late 1970s that made *The Wall*? Or is it the group of musicians, writers, and producer who, under David Gilmour's guidance, put together one of the most successful tours of the late 1980s?

Perhaps all of the above. In any case, like only the best popular music, the work of Pink Floyd, now dating back more than 25 years, continues to speak to generations of listeners, whether the people who made it have turned into recluses or not, whether they get along with each other or not, whatever they're allowed to call themselves, and whatever happens next.

# *Discography*

## U.K. RELEASES

### SINGLES

| Record Label | Record Number | Title | Release Date |
|---|---|---|---|
| Columbia | DB 8156 | Arnold Layne/Candy and a Currant Bun | 11 Mar 1967 |
| Columbia | DB 8214 | See Emily Play/ Scarecrow | 16 Jun 1967 |
| Columbia | DB 8310 | Apples and Oranges/Paint Box | 18 Nov 1967 |
| Columbia | DB 8410 | It Would Be So Nice/Julia Dream | 12 Apr 1968 |
| Columbia | DB 8511 | Point Me at the Sky/Careful With That Axe, Eugene | 17 Dec 1968 |
| Harvest | HAR 5194 | Another Brick in the Wall, Part Two/One of My Turns | 16 Nov 1979 |
| Harvest | HAR 5222 | When the Tigers Break Free/Bring the Boys Back Home | 26 Jul 1982 |
| Harvest | HAR 5224 | Not Now John/The Hero's Return – Parts One and Two | Apr 1983 |
| EMI | CDEM26 | Learning to Fly/One Slip/Terminal Frost/ Terminal Frost | 1987 |
| EMI | EM34 | On the Turning Away/Run Like Hell | 1987 |

### ALBUMS

| Record Label | Record Number | Title | Release Date |
|---|---|---|---|
| Columbia | SCX 6157 | The Piper at the Gates of Dawn | 5 Aug 1967 |
| Columbia | SCX 6258 | A Saucerful of Secrets | 29 Jun 1968 |
| Instant | INLP 002 | Tonite Let's All Make Love in London | 1968 |
| Columbia | SCX 6346 | More | Jul 1969 |
| Harvest | SHDW 1/2 | Ummagumma | 25 Oct 1969 |
| M.G.M. | 2315 002 | Zabriskie Point | Mar 1970 |
| Harvest | SHVL 78 | Atom Heart Mother | 10 Oct 1970 |
| EMI Starline | SRS 5071 | Relics | May 1971 |
| Harvest | SHVL 795 | Meddle | Nov 1971 |
| Harvest | SHSP 4020 | Obscured by Clouds | 3 Jun 1972 |
| Harvest | SHVL 804 | The Dark Side of the Moon | Mar 1973 |
| Harvest | SHDW 403 | A Nice Pair | Dec 1973 |
| Harvest | SHVL 814 | Wish You Were Here | 15 Sep 1975 |
| Harvest | SHVL 815 | Animals | 23 Jan 1977 |
| Harvest | SHDW 411 | The Wall | 30 Nov 1979 |
| Harvest | SHVL 822 | A Collection of Great Dance Songs | 21 Nov 1981 |
| Harvest | SHPF 1983 | The Final Cut | 21 Mar 1983 |
| EMI | EMD 1003 | A Momentary Lapse of Reason | 7 Sep 1987 |

### SOLO RECORDINGS

**Syd Barrett**

*Singles*

| | | | |
|---|---|---|---|
| Harvest | | Octopus/Golden Hair | Dec 1969 |

*Albums*

| | | | |
|---|---|---|---|
| Harvest | SHVL 765 | The Madcap Laughs | Jan 1970 |
| Harvest | SHSP 4007 | Barrett | Nov 1970 |
| Strange Fruit | SFPS 043 | The Peel Session | Feb 1988 |
| Harvest | SHSP 4126 | Opel | Oct 1988 |

## David Gilmour

### Singles

| Record Label | Record Number | Title | Release Date |
|---|---|---|---|
| Harvest | HAR 5167 | There's No Way Out of Here/Deafinitely | 4 Aug 1978 |
| Harvest | HAR 5226 | Blue Light/Cruise | 13 Feb 1984 |
| Harvest | HAR 5229 | Love on the Air/Let's Get Metaphysical | 27 Apr 1984 |

### Albums

| | | | |
|---|---|---|---|
| Harvest | SHVL 817 | David Gilmour | 25 May 1978 |
| Harvest | SHSP 24-0079-1 | About Face | 5 Mar 1984 |

## Nick Mason

### Singles

| | | | |
|---|---|---|---|
| Harvest | HAR 5238 | Lie for a Lie/And the Address | 22 Sep 1985 |

### Albums

| | | | |
|---|---|---|---|
| Harvest | SHSP 4116 | Nick Mason's Fictitious Sports | May 1980 |
| Harvest | MAF 1 | Profiles (by Mason & Fenn) | 19 Aug 1985 |

## Roger Waters

### Singles

| | | | |
|---|---|---|---|
| Harvest | HAR 5228 | 5.01 am (The Pros and Cons of Hitch Hiking)/4.30 (Apparently They Were Traveling Abroad) | 9 Apr 1984 |
| Harvest | HAR 5230 | 5.06 am (Every Stranger's Eyes/4.39 am (For the First Time Today) | Jun 1984 |
| Harvest | EM6 | Radio Waves/Going to Live in L.A. | 11 May 1987 |
| EMI | EM37 | The Tide Is Turning (After Live Aid)/Get Back to Radio | 16 Nov 1987 |

### Albums

| | | | |
|---|---|---|---|
| Harvest | SHSP 4008 | Music from the Body (with Ron Geesin) | Dec 1970 |
| Harvest | SHVL 24 0105 1 | The Pros and Cons of Hitch Hiking | 8 May 1984 |
| Virgin | V2406 | When the Wind Blows | Oct 1986 |
| EMI | KAOS 1 | Radio K.A.O.S | 15 Jun 1987 |
| Columbia | 468761 | Amused to Death | Sep 1992 |

## Rick Wright

### Singles

| | | | |
|---|---|---|---|
| Harvest | HAR 5227 | Confusion/Eyes of a Gypsy (by Zee) | 12 Mar 1984 |

### Albums

| | | | |
|---|---|---|---|
| Harvest | SHVL 818 | Wet Dream | 1978 |
| Harvest | SHSP 24 0101 1 | Identity (by Zee) | 9 Apr 1984 |

# U.S. RELEASES

## Singles

| Record Label | Record Number | Title | Release Date |
|---|---|---|---|
| Tower | 333 | Arnold Layne/Candy and a Currant Bun | 1967 |
| Tower | 356 | See Emily Play/Scarecrow | 1967 |
| Tower | 378 | Flaming/The Gnome | 1967 |
| Tower | 428 | Julia Dream/It Would Be So Nice | 1968 |
| Tower | 440 | Remember a Day/Let There Be More Light | 1968 |
| Harvest | 3240 | One of These Days/Fearless | 1971 |
| Harvest | 3391 | Free Four/Stay | 1972 |
| Harvest | 3609 | Money/Any Color You Like | 1973 |
| Harvest | 3832 | Us and Them/Time | 1973 |
| Columbia | 3-10248 | Have a Cigar/Welcome to the Machine | 1975 |
| Columbia | 1-11187 | Another Brick in the Wall, Part Two/One of My Turns | 1979 |
| Columbia | 1-11265 | Run Like Hell/Don't Leave Me Now | 1980 |
| Columbia | 1-11311 | Comfortably Numb/Hey You | 1980 |
| Columbia | 18-03142 | When the Tigers Broke Free/Bring the Boys Back Home | 1982 |
| Columbia | 38-03905 | Not Now John/The Hero's Return — Parts One and Two | 1983 |
| Columbia | 38-07363 | Learning to Fly/Terminal Frost | 1987 |

## Albums

| Record Label | Record Number | Title | Release Date |
|---|---|---|---|
| Tower | ST 5903 | Pink Floyd | Sep 1967 |
| Tower | ST 5131 | A Saucerful of Secrets | Jul 1968 |
| Tower | ST 5169 | More | Jul 1969 |
| Harvest | STBB 388 | Ummagumma | Nov 1969 |
| M.G.M. | SE-4668ST | Zabriskie Point | Jan 1970 |
| Harvest | SKAO 382 | Atom Heart Mother | Oct 1970 |
| Harvest | SW 759 | Relics | May 1971 |
| Harvest | SMAS 832 | Meddle | Nov 1971 |
| Harvest | ST 11078 | Obscured by Clouds | Jun 1972 |
| Harvest | SMAS 11163 | The Dark Side of the Moon | Mar 1973 |
| Tower | SABB 11257 | A Nice Pair | Dec 1973 |
| Columbia | PC 33453 | Wish You Were Here | Sep 1975 |
| Columbia | JC 34474 | Animals | 23 Jan 1977 |
| Columbia | PC2 36183 | The Wall | Nov 1979 |
| Columbia | TC 37680 | A Collection of Great Dance Songs | Nov 1981 |
| Columbia | QC 38243 | The Final Cut | Mar 1983 |
| Capitol | ST 12276 | Works | 1983 |
| Columbia | CK 40599 | A Momentary Lapse of Reason | Sep 1987 |
| Columbia | C2K 44484 | Delicate Sound of Thunder | 26 Nov 1988 |
| Polydor | 847 042-2 | Knebworth: The Album | 1990 |

**SOLO RECORDINGS**

**Syd Barrett**

*Albums*

| Record Label | Record Number | Title | Release Date |
|---|---|---|---|
| Harvest | SABB 11314 | Syd Barrett | 1974 |
| Capitol | C2 91206 | Opel | 1988 |

**David Gilmour**

*Albums*

| | | | |
|---|---|---|---|
| Columbia | JC 35388 | David Gilmour | 1978 |
| Columbia | FC 39396 | About Face | 1984 |

**Nick Mason**

*Albums*

| | | | |
|---|---|---|---|
| Columbia | FC 37307 | Nick Mason's Fictitious Sports | 1981 |
| Columbia | CK 40142 | Profiles (by Mason & Fenn) | 1985 |

**Roger Waters**

*Albums*

| | | | |
|---|---|---|---|
| Columbia | FC 39290 | The Pros and Cons of Hitch Hiking | Apr 1984 |
| Columbia | CK 40795 | Radio K.A.O.S. | 15 Jun 1987 |
| Restless Retro | 7 72395-2 | Music from the Body (with Ron Geesin) | 1990 |
| Mercury | 846 611-2 | The Wall Live in Berlin | 1990 |
| Columbia | CK 47127 | Used to Death | Sep 1992 |

**Rick Wright**

*Albums*

| | | | |
|---|---|---|---|
| Columbia | JC 35559 | Wet Dream | 1978 |

# Index